1. Prologue

I0435293

THERE is perhaps nothing extraordinary in the fact that man is wise and just, takes great care to provide for his own children, -shows due consideration for his parents, seeks sustenance for himself, protects himself against plots, and possesses all the other gifts of nature which are his. For man has been endowed with speech, of all things the most precious, and has been granted reason, which is of the greatest help and use.

Moreover, he knows how to reverence and worship the gods. But that dumb animals should by nature possess some good quality and should have many of man's amazing excellences assigned to them along with man, is indeed a remarkable fact. And to know accurately the special characteristics of each, and how living creatures also have been a source of interest no less than man, demands a trained intelligence and much learning. Now I am well aware of the labour that others have expended on this subject, yet I have collected all the materials that I could; I have clothed them in untechnical language, and am persuaded that my achievement is a treasure far from negligible. So if anyone considers them profitable, let him make use of them; anyone who does not consider them so may give them to his father to keep and attend to.

For not all things give pleasure to all men, nor do all men consider all subjects worthy of study. Although I was born later than many accomplished writers of an earlier day, the accident of date ought not to mulct me of praise, if I too produce a learned work whose ampler research and whose choice of language make it deserving of serious attention.

Mythology, mariners' yarns, vulgar superstitions, the ascertained facts of nature—all serve to adorn a tale and, on occasion, to point a moral. His religion is the popular stoicism of the age. Aleian repeatedly affirms his belief in the gods and in divine providence; the wisdom and beneficence of Nature are held up to veneration; the folly and selfishness of man are contrasted with the untaught virtues of the animal world. Some animals, to be sure, have their failings, but he chooses rather to dwell upon their good qualities, devotion, courage, self-sacrifice, gratitude. Again, animals are guided by reason, and from them we may learn contentment, control of the passions, and calm in the face of death.

Animal Peculiarity Volume 2 Part 8

By T.P Just

~~~

Copyright © 2012 by T.P Just. All rights reserved.

All Rights Reserved. No part of this publication may be reproduced in any form or by any means, including scanning, photocopying, or otherwise without prior written permission of the copyright holder.

This eBook is licensed for your personal enjoyment only. This eBook may not be re-sold or given away to other people. If you would like to share this book with another person, please purchase an additional copy for each recipient. Get All The Books In The Series:

Animal Peculiarity Volume 1 [1-8]
Animal Peculiarity Volume 2 [1-8]
Just Enterprises

Table of Contents

2. Tame Crocodiles

I have heard that the Egyptians assert that the sacred Crocodiles are tame, and if their keepers at any rate touch and handle them they submit and do not object; and they keep their jaws open when the keepers insert their hands and cleanse their teeth and pick out bits of flesh that have got between them.

Further, the Egyptians assert that the aforesaid Crocodiles are endowed with prophecy, and adduce the following evidence. Ptolemy (which of the line it was, you must ask them) was calling to the tamest of the Crocodiles, but it paid no attention and would not accept the food he offered.

And the priests realised that the Crocodile knew that Ptolemy's end was approaching and consequently declined to take food from him.

3. Divination by Fishes

I have heard that some people practice divination by birds and devote themselves to their study and scrutinise their flight and the quarters of the sky where they appear. And seers like Teiresias, Polydamas, Polyeidus, Theoclymenus and many another are celebrated for their knowledge of this art, while men such as Silanus, Megistias, Euclides and the long tale of their successors were skilled in deciding upon the dispositions of entrails.

Again, I have heard people assert that some divine by means of barley-corns, of sieves, and of small cheeses. And I have ascertained that there is a village in Lycia between Myra and Phellus called Sura where there are those who devote themselves to divination by means of fish.

And they understand what it purports if the fish come at their call or withdraw, and what it signifies if they pay no attention, and what it portends if they come in numbers.

And you shall hear these prophetic utterances of the sages when a fish leaps out of the water or comes floating up from the depths, and when it accepts the food or on the other hand rejects it.

4. Hunters and Hunted

It seems that donkeys are easily overcome and seized by wolves, and bees by bee-eaters, cicadas by swallows, and snakes by deer. And the leopard captures most animals, especially the monkey, by its odour.

5. Animals poisonous to the touch

From Megasthenes I learn that a small fish occurs in the Indian Ocean, and that when alive it is invisible, since presumably it swims down in the depths, but that when dead it floats to the surface.

Anyone who touches it faints to begin with and later on dies. And if one treads upon the chelydrus even without being bitten, as Apollodorus says in his work Of Poisonous Animals, death is inevitable.

For he says that mere contact with the creature produces sepsis. And what is more, if anyone tries to administer medical treatment or help of any kind to the dying man he gets blisters on his hands, simply from having touched the man who trod on the snake.

And Aristoxenus says somewhere that a man killed a snake with his hands and, though unbitten died notwithstanding. And his very clothes which he happened to be wearing at the time when he slew the snake, turned in a short while to putrefaction.

The Amphisbaena

Nicander asserts that the slough of the Amphisbaena if wrapped round a walking-stick drives away all snakes and other creatures which kill not by biting but by striking.

6. The Dog and its medicines

A Dog burdened with a full stomach knows of a herb that grows on dry stone walls, and if he eats it he vomits all that is paining him, mixed with phlegm and bile, and a great deal of excrement also passes off; so he restores his health without any need of medical assistance.

Further, he voids a quantity of black bile which if retained causes madness, a trouble- some disease in Dogs. And when infected by Worms Dogs eat the awns of corn, according to Aristotle.

When wounded they have their tongue as a medicine, and with their tongue they lick the wounded place and restore it to a healthy condition; bandages, compresses, and the compounding of medicines they scorn.

And another thing which Dogs have not failed to observe is that the fruit of the . . . fattens swine indeed but causes Dogs a pain in their haunches.

And though a Dog may see a sow gorging itself with the aforesaid fruit, with great self-control it leaves it to the sow for all its seeming sweetness. Men however yield to those who prevail upon them to eat against their will, often to an altogether immoderate degree.

7. An Elephant hunt

Elephants would not easily fail to notice an ambush. For instance, when they come near to the pit which elephant-hunters are in the habit of secretly digging, whether by some natural instinct or by some altogether mysterious faculty of divination they restrain themselves from going any further, and turn back and put up a most strenuous resistance as in war and try to overthrow their hunters and, thrusting their way through them, to seek safety in flight after overcoming their adversaries.

So then there ensues a fierce battle and there is a slaughter of hunters and hunted. And this is how the battle is fought. The men take aim and hurl stout spears at them, while the Elephants seize upon any man that has fallen in their way, dash him to earth, trample upon him, and wounding him with their tusks inflict upon him a most pitiful and agonizing death.

And the animals attack, their ears in passion spread wide like sails, after the manner of ostriches which open their wings to flee or to attack. And the Elephants bending their trunk inwards and folding it beneath their tusks, like the ram of a ship driving along with a great surge, fall upon the men in a tremendous charge, overturning many and bellowing with a piercing, shrill note like a trumpet.

And as those who are caught are trampled or smashed by the beasts' knees, a great sound of bones being crushed can be heard even at a distance, and men's faces, with eyes knocked out, nose battered, and forehead split, lose their distinctive features, and frequently become unrecognisable even by their nearest relatives.

Others however escape contrary to expectation, in the following manner. A hunter has been caught, but the Elephant in its forward rush has over passed him and has planted its knees upon the earth and has besides fixed its tusks in a thicket or in a tree- root or some similar object, and is held fast and can only with difficulty Withdraw and pull them out. Meanwhile the hunter slips out and escapes. In such a battle therefore it often happens that the Elephants are victorious, often however that they are defeated through the men designedly applying various means of scaring them.

For instance, trumpets are sounded; the hunters make a din and a clash by beating their spears on their shields; now they light a fire on the ground, now they lift it up in the air; or again they launch burning firebrands like javelins and violently brandish great torches in full blaze before the faces of the animals.

And as the animals dread and are dazzled by these things they are pushed back and sometimes forced to fall into the pit which till then they have kept clear of.

8. Love of beauty in animals

Hegemon in his poem, the Dardanica, among other things touching Aleuas the Thessalian, says that a snake was enamored of him. And when he says that this Aleuas had 'golden' hair he is romancing; let me call it 'flaxen.' And he says that he was a neatherd on mount Ossa, as Anchises was on Ida, and that he pastured his cattle near the spring called Haemonia.

(The spring also would be in Thessaly.) Now a snake of enormous size fell in love with Aleuas and crept up to him and kissed his hair and with its tongue licked and washed the face of its loved one and brought him as presents many of the spoils of its hunting.

Now if a ram was overcome by love of Glance the harpist, and a dolphin of a youth at GIassus, what is, there to prevent a snake also from falling in love with a handsome shepherd, or the most keen-sighted of creatures from being a good judge of conspicuous beauty?

So it seems that it is in fact a characteristic of animals to fall in love not only with their companions and kin but even with those who bear no relation to them at all but are yet beautiful.

9. The 'Sibritae' scorpions

I have heard that in Ethiopia the 'Scorpions known as Sibritae (that is what the inhabitants commonly call them, as is natural) feed upon lizards, asps, sphondylae cockroaches, and all creeping things, but I have ascertained that anyone who treads upon their excrement develops ulcers.

10. Various Snakes

In Corcyra there occur water-snakes, as they are called which round upon their pursuers and by blasts of foul breath make them pause in their attack and deter them. According to one account the Typhlops (blind-eyes), which people also call Typhline and Cophias as well, has a head nearly resembling the moray, but very small eyes.

And the second of its two names, that is Cophias, it has derived from the fact that it is dull of hearing. But its skin is hard and takes a long time to cut through. And the Acontias (javelin-snake), they say, is amphibious and spends much time on dry land, lying in wait for every kind of living creature. And it shows skill in its fell designs, thus. It lurks hidden it may be in thoroughfares ; often it crawls up some tree and coils itself up and concealing its head in its coils, spies quietly upon the passers-by.

Then it launches itself on whatever is passing, be it brute beast or man. The creature is good at leaping and is capable of jumping as much as twenty cubits, if need be. And where it leaps it instantly fastens on.

11. Wolves and Ox

If by chance Wolves come upon an Ox that has fallen into a deep pond, they harass and terrify him from the bank, never allowing him to swim across and get out on to land, and compel him after long torment and floundering to drown. Then the strongest Wolf in the pack leaps into the water and swimming up to the Ox, seizes its tail and begins to drag it to the bank; and a second wolf seizes the tail of the first and drags it, then a third drags the second, and a fourth the third, and this is repeated up to the last Wolf, which is standing out of the water.

And having hauled out the Ox in this way, they enjoy a feast. They lie in wait for a strayed Calf and leap upon it and seizing it by the nose drag it along. But the Calf pulls against them and there is a fierce struggle for it, the Wolves trying to overcome it by force, the Calf fighting hard not to yield.

And when they see it resisting with all its might in this way, they let go; whereupon the Calf by straining in the opposite direction is upset, and the Wolves leap upon it, tear open its belly, and devour it.

12. Elephants cross a ditch

When Elephants are unable to cross a ditch the largest one in the herd throws himself into it and standing transversely bridges the gap, while the rest tread on his back, cross to the far side, and make off, but not until they have rescued him. And the way in which they rescue him is as follows. One of them on the bank puts his foot forward and allows the large Elephant to wrap his trunk round it. Meantime the others throw undergrowth and timber into the trench as fast as they can. And he mounts on these and clinging firmly with all his might to the 0ther's foot is drawn up without difficulty. There is in India a tract of land called Phalacra (bald). And the reason for the name is that any creature which eats the grass growing there loses its hair and its horns. Accordingly Elephants do not willingly go near this tract, but if they have drawn near to it they move away, since Elephants, like prudent men, avoid anything that is harmful.

13. The Sponge

The Sponge is directed by a small animal resembling a spider rather than a crab. For the Sponge is no lifeless or bloodless object engendered by the sea, but clings to the rocks like other creatures and has a certain power of movement in itself, though it needs, as you might say, someone to remind it that it is a living creature, for owing to some natural porosity it remains motionless and at rest, until something encounters its pores; then the spider-like creature pricks it, and it seizes what has fallen in and makes a meal. But when a man approaches to cut it off, the Sponge is pricked by the animal that lives in it, shudders, and contracts, and the trouble and labour that this causes to the fisherman is considerable, and no mistake.

14. The Elephant, its continence

I have indeed spoken of Elephants in a separate chapter, but I shall add the following . . . it is most fitting to state that they have been gifted with temperance. For they seek intercourse with the female not as though minded to commit an outrage or from lust, but like men desiring a succession to their family and to beget children, in order that their common offspring may not fail but that they may leave their seed after them. At any rate once only in a life-time do their thoughts turn to love, when the female herself submits. Then when each one has impregnated its mate, thereafter it knows her no more. And they do not couple without reserve or in the sight of others but withdraw and screen themselves in thick trees or in some close- growing forest or in some deep hollow, which affords them ample means of hiding.

Now I said above that they were just, and I have already spoken of their valour. Their continence has been displayed in the present instance. Further, anyone who has leisure to learn of their detestation of evil should lend an ear and listen to this. The trainer of a tame Elephant had a somewhat elderly but rich wife. Now he was in love with another woman, and desiring that his wife's property should become hers, he strangled his wife and buried her, rash man that he was, close by the Elephants manger, and married the other woman.

Reveals murder

So then the Elephant seizing hold of the new arrival with its trunk led her up to the dead body, dug it up, and laid it bare with its tusks, showing by its mere action what it could not express in words, and enlightening the woman as to the conduct of him who had wedded her; such was the Elephant's hatred of evil.

15. The Anchovy

Anchovies (engrauleis, which some call encrasicholi and I have even heard a third name applied to them, for some call them 'wolf-mouths') are a tiny fish, prolific by nature, and pure white in appearance.

They are principally eaten by fish which swim in shoals, and so when scared they rush to one another, and as each clings to its neighbor, by their close cohesion they avoid falling an easy prey to plots upon their life.

And so united is their mass when they have rushed together that even ships which run into them do not cleave it. Moreover should someone wish to drive an oar or a pole through them, they are not torn apart, but cling to each other as though woven together.

But if you put your hand down and pull hard as if you were drawing grains of wheat or beans from a heap, you may catch some, with the result that they are often torn to pieces and that fragments of fish are caught, while the rest is left behind.

For though you may get possession of the tail, yet the head remains with the other fish; or you may take home a head, but the rest of the fish remains in the sea. Their swimming in a dense, compact mass is called a 'draught,' and a single draught often fills fifty fishing-boats, as toilers of the sea inform us.

16. Pigs and pirates

The Sow recognises the voice of the swineherd, and attends to his call even though it has wandered away. Evidence for this statement is to hand. Some miscreants beached their pirate vessel on the shore of Etruria, and proceeding inland came upon a fold belonging to some swineherds and containing a large number of Sows.

These they seized, put them on board, loosed their cables, and continued on their voyage. Now so long as the pirates were on the spot the swineherds kept quiet, but when they were off shore in the roadstead 'and as far as a cry might carry,' then the swineherds with their accustomed cry called the Swine back to them.

And when the Swine heard it they pressed together to one side of the vessel and capsized it. And the miscreants were drowned forthwith, but the Swine swam away to their masters.

17. A Stork punishes adulteress

They say that the Stork also is subject to jealousy. "At any rate at Crannon in Thessaly a man who had married a beautiful wife of the name of Alcinoe left her at home and went away on his travels.

So Alcinoe had intercourse with one of the servants. The Stork that was about the house got to know of this and would not tolerate it, but avenged its master. At any rate it sprang upon the woman and blinded her eyes.

I have earlier on spoken of jealousy on the part of a Purple Coot, then of a Dog in like case, and now of a Stork equally affected over a marriage that went wrong.

18. Waters that change the colour of sheep

Sheep change their colour as their drink varies with the character of the rivers. The season of the year in which this occurs is the season of mating. So from being white they become black and the contrary change of colour occurs.
This commonly takes place near the river of Antandria and the river in Thrace whose name the neighboring Thracians will tell you.
And since the Scamander in the Troad turns the sheep that drink of it yellow, the colour which the flocks acquire has caused the name Xanthus (yellow) to be added to its original name of 'Scamander.

19. Woman of Tarentum and Stork

In this respect also animals are good, viz at remembering to be grateful. There was a woman in Tarentum, admirable in other ways and particularly as a faithful wife. Her name was Heracleis. So long as her husband lived she cared for him with the utmost devotion.

But when he died the woman took a dislike to life in the city and to the home in which she had seen her husband dead, and such was her grief that she went to dwell among the tombs and was content to remain by her late husband's sepulchre, constant to him who was beneath the soil.

And once in summer when some storks, still fledglings, were essaying their first flight, one of them, the youngest, not having sufficient strength of wing, fell and broke one of its legs. So Heracleis seeing its fall and finding how its leg was injured, took pity on the nestling and picking it up very gently wrapped up the wound, and tended it with fomentations and plasters, brought it food, gave it drink, and, when in due course it was strong and had grown its quill- feathers, set it free.

And the stork, knowing by some strange instinct that it owed her the price of its life, departed. Later when a year had passed and spring was just beginning to brighten, the woman chanced to be warming herself in the sun, and the Stork which had been healed by her, seeing its benefactress, checked the speed of its wings and sinking nearer to earth came close, opened its bill, and disgorged a stone into the lap of Heracleis, and then flew off and settled on the roof.

At first, naturally enough, she was amazed and startled out of her wits, and was at a loss to conjecture what this action could mean. And so she put the stone away somewhere indoors; later being woken in the night she saw that it diffused brightness and a gleam, and the house was lit up as though a torch had been brought in, so strong radiance came from, and was engendered by, the lump of stone.

And when she had taken hold of the Stork and handled it she recognised the scar left by the wound, and knew that it was the very bird which had been the object of her pity and her ministrations.

20. The Smooth Lobster

If you catch a Smooth Lobster and remove it to a great distance, leaving a mark at the place where you caught it, you will find the self-same Lobster at the spot where it was captured: I mean, if you take it along the seashore and put it down somewhere near enough for it to be able to crawl into the sea.

21. The Indian Mynah

Hunter' is its name; Nature has given it wings; it is allied to the tribe of thrushes; its colour is black; it has a musical voice. And it is called 'the Hunter,' and rightly so; for with its song it captivates the small birds that fly to it beneath the spell of its sweet music.

Knowing therefore the natural advantage that it possesses, it appears to employ this gift of Nature to please itself and also to feed itself, for it delights to listen to its own voice, and pursues the birds that approach it and takes its fill of them. Anyone who hunts this bird and confines it in a cage, gets nothing for his pains, for he possesses a bird that refuses to sing, seeming by its silence to punish its captor for en- slaving it.

22. The Egyptian Plover

I have spoken above of the benefit which the Egyptian Plovers confer upon Crocodiles, and Herodotus mentions it in his Account of Egypt. But what I did not mention, though I knew it, I will mention now, in order that others also may learn the facts.

The Egyptian Plover is one of the marsh-fowls and ranges along the banks of rivers, feeding upon whatever it chances to pick up here and there, while the Crocodile provides it with the food that I spoke of. And the bird repays it by taking care of it and keeping watch on its behalf while it sleeps.

For as it lies asleep the Ichneumon has designs upon it, and fastening on its throat has often throttled it. But the Egyptian Plover utters its cry, beats the Crocodile on the nose, rouses it, and eggs it on against its enemy.

Now whether we should applaud the bird for its solicitude on behalf of an omnivorous and gluttonous animal, we shall know later. It is the special characteristics of these creatures that I have mentioned.

23. The Sting-ray

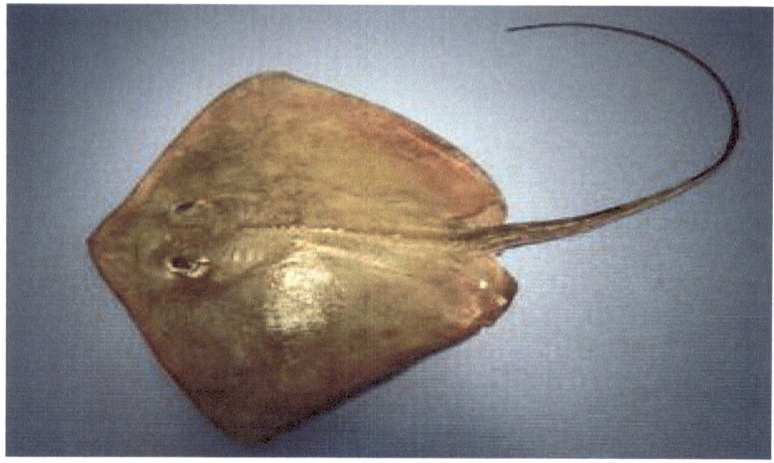

The Trygon (I am not speaking of the one that lives in the air [i.e. the Turtle-dove] but of the one in the sea [i.e. the Sting-ray]) swims when it wants to, or again raises itself and flies. Its sting, of which I have spoken above, is deadly.

Yet that it should sting brute beasts and men and kill them on the spot is no matter for wonder. But what is startling is this which I am about to mention.

If you apply the sting to the largest tree when in a thriving state, flourishing, and in full foliage, and stab the tree, in a short while it sheds its leaves, and as they floats down to earth the entire stem withers and seems as though scorched by the sun.

24. The Young Elephant

An Elephant emerges head first at birth, and the size of it when born is that of the largest sucking- pig. Several small Elephants follow a single mother, so they say. And if you want to touch the little ones when new-born, the mothers do not resent it but permit it.

For they know that no one will lay hands on them to do them harm or punish them, but that everyone has kindly intentions and would pet them. For who would hurt such a little creature?

But when they are hunted and fall into the pit and see that there is no escape for them, they forget thee spirit that possessed them when they were free and readily go for any food that is held out to them and drink the water that is offered, and if wine is poured into their trunks they do not refuse that loving-cup.

25. The Sturgeon

Our great poet is supposed to call the Sturgeon a 'sacred fish'.
According to one account it is rare, but is caught in the sea off
Pamphylia, though even there hardly at all.
But if it is caught, the fisherman deck themselves with
garlands to celebrate their good luck; they garland the fishing-
boats as well, and put into port, as with cymbals and flutes
they summon people to bear witness to their catch.

26. The Anthias

Others however consider that the Anthias, and not this fish, is sacred. And the reason is that in whatever part of the sea it appears, that spot is presumably bound to be free from savage creatures and there is peace between fish and everything that seeks its prey in the waters, while the fish themselves bring forth their young without fear.

But it is no business of mine to explore the mysteries of Nature, and rightly so, since the lion goes in fear of the cock, and so does the basilisk, moreover the elephant dreads a pig. But those who have much leisure to spend in seeking the reasons for these things will take no account of time, and for all that, will never come to the end of their researches.

Get All The Books In The Series:

Animal Peculiarity Volume 1 [1-8]
Animal Peculiarity Volume 2 [1-8]

www.ingramcontent.com/pod-product-compliance
Lightning Source LLC
Chambersburg PA
CBHW040316010626
45792CB00022B/591